Itty Bitty Knitties™

Designs by Frances Hughes and Sue Childress

HOUSE of
WHITE
BIRCHES

PUBLISHERS
SINCE 1947

Table of Contents

Hooray for the Team,
page 4

Maid of Honor,
page 14

Sailor Boy,
page 19

Moses Basket & Layette,
page 16

Fun in the Sun,
page 24

Introduction

Knitters of all skill levels will love making these cute-as-can-be outfits for adorable 5-inch dolls. Some of the projects to follow include the bride & groom, cheerleader, baseball player and more. Knit her and him outfits for sleepy time, including a security blanket, or a Moses basket and layette for Dolly's little nap.

Each ensemble is made using simple knit and purl techniques. All patterns conveniently call for size #2 needles and crochet yarn. All 11 projects are rated Easy, making them perfect for beginner and novice knitters, and doll clothes are a great way to learn simple shaping techniques on a small scale. You'll enjoy making these darling little outfits, with matching accessories such as booties, headbands, caps and panties, too!

Meet the Designers

Frances Hughes

I was born in a small town in East Texas, and I am 75 years young. My husband and I have been married since 1952. We have two sons, nine adult grandchildren and eight great-grandchildren.

I learned to crochet at a very young age. Being left-handed made this a challenge, but the rewards far outweighed the effort it took. Then, much later in life, I learned to knit. Knitting opened up a whole new way of expressing myself through my needlecrafting, broadening my horizons.

My sister Sue and I opened a yarn shop in 1984. It has been plenty of fun and quite a bit of work, but I love it all. I sold my first design to Annie's Attic in 1984 after telling Sue that if she could do that, I could too.

Sue and I have had designs published by Annie's Attic, Needlecraft Shop, House of White Birches and Leisure Arts. My designs have also been in several magazines, including *Knitting Digest, Creative Knitting, Crochet World, Old-Time Crochet, McCalls, Country Woman* and *Ribbon Works*.

Sue Childress

I was born in a very small town to a mother who loved crafts and crochet. I've been married to Robert since 1957. We have two children and five grandchildren.

When my children were small, I would ask them if they liked what I was making. If they said no, then I would never make that item again. When my sister Frances and I were attending craft fairs, my daughter was a good gauge for us. If she liked a project, it was always a best-seller.

My sister and I opened Stitches 'N Stuff Yarn and Gift Shop in 1984. I have enjoyed being a part of the yarn industry with all its ups and downs. I never get tired of all the wonderful yarns and notions that have flooded our world over the last few years.

I've known how to crochet since I was a little girl, but I didn't learn to knit until I was 54. I've enjoyed knitting as much as crocheting. It's much more fun to know how to do both!

Hooray for the Team

Designs by Sue Childress

Skill Level
 EASY

Size
Fits 5-inch doll

Materials
- Omega Crys (sock weight; 68% acrylic/32% polyester; 287 yds/40g per ball): 50 yds each red #241 (A) and white #200 (B)
- Size 2 (2.75mm) needles or size needed to obtain gauge
- 2 snaps
- Sewing needle and matching thread
- 2-inch square of cardboard

Gauge
8 sts = 1 inch in garter st.
To save time, take time to check gauge.

Special Abbreviation
Knit in front and back (kfb): Inc by knitting in front and back of next st.

Dress

Skirt
Note: Skirt is worked side to side.

With A, cast on 10 sts.

*With A, knit 10 rows; with B, knit 10 rows; rep from * 4 more times.

Bind off.

Bodice
With A, pick up and knit 54 sts along 1 long side of skirt.

Row 1: K2tog, *k2, k2tog; rep from * across—40 sts.

Row 2: K8, bind off 4 sts for armhole, k16 (includes st on needle after bind-off), bind-off 4 sts for armhole, k8 (includes st on needle after bind-off)—32 sts.

Row 3: K8, cast on 4 sts, k1, k2tog, k4, k2tog, k4, k2tog, k1, cast on 4 sts, k8—37 sts.

Row 4: K13, k2tog, k7, k2tog, k13—35 sts.

Bind off.

Sew back skirt seam, leaving ¾ inch open at neck edge.

Sew snap at neck edge.

Panties

With B, cast on 10 sts.

Rows 1–16: *K1, p1; rep from * across—crotch formed.

Next row: Cast on 12 sts, k12 cast-on sts, [k1, p1] 5 times across crotch, cast-on 12 sts—34 sts.

Next row: K12, [k1, p1] 5 times, k12.

Rep last row 7 times.

Bind off.

Fold ends of last 8 rows tog to meet at center back and sew to cast-on edge of crotch. Sew snap at top of opening.

Shoes

With B, cast on 14 sts.

Row 1: Knit across.

Row 2: K5, kfb of each of next 4 sts, k5—18 sts.

Row 3: K6, [p2tog] 3 times, k6—15 sts.

Row 4: K5, p2tog, p1, p2tog, k5—13 sts.

Bind off.

Sew back and bottom seam.

Cut 6-inch length of A. Beg and ending at center front weave through top edge and tie ends in bow.

Pompoms
Make 2

Holding A and B tog, wrap 40 times around 2-inch square of cardboard. Cut an 8-inch length each of red and white, tie in middle. Cut yarn ends and trim even. Tie off 8-inch length leaving enough to go around doll's arms.

Headband

With B, cast on 40 sts.

Rows 1–3: *K1, p1; rep from * across.

Bind off.

Sew ends tog.

Pompom: Holding A and B tog, wrap 15 times around 2 fingers; tie in center. Cut ends and trim even. Tie to headband.

Practice Mat

Note: *Color not in use may be carried along the edge or cut and joined for each stripe.*

With A, cast on 18 sts.

*With A, knit 10 rows; with B, knit 10 rows; rep from * 4 more times.

Bind off. ❖

Sleepy Time

Designs by Sue Childress

Skill Level

 EASY

Size

Fits 5-inch doll

Materials

- Omega Crys (sock weight; 68% acrylic/ 32% polyester; 287 yds/40g per ball): 100 yds mint #221 (MC), 15 yds white #200 (CC)
- Size 2 (2.75mm) needles or size needed to obtain gauge
- 3 snaps
- 12 inches ⅛-inch-wide white ribbon
- Sewing needle and matching thread

1 SUPER FINE

Gauge

8 sts = 1 inch in St st.
To save time, take time to check gauge.

Special Abbreviation

Knit in front and back (kfb): Inc by knitting in front and back of next st.

Shirt

Body

Note: Body is made in one piece to armholes, then divided to work fronts and back.

With CC, cast on 38 sts.

Rows 1–3: Knit across. Cut CC.

Row 4 (RS): With MC, k2, *p2, k2; rep from * across.

Row 5: P2, *k2, p2; rep from * across.

Rows 6–9: Rep [Rows 4 and 5] twice.

Right Front

Row 1 (RS): K2, [p2, k2] twice—10 sts.

Row 2: P2, [k2, p2] twice.

Rows 3–6: Rep [Rows 1 and 2] twice.

Bind off.

Back

With RS facing, join MC in next st.

Row 1 (RS): P2, [k2, p2] 4 times—18 sts.

Row 2: K2, [p2, k2] 4 times.

Rows 3–6: Rep [Rows 1 and 2] twice.

Bind off.

Left Front

With RS facing, join MC in next st.

Row 1 (RS): K2, [p2, k2] twice—10 sts.

Row 2: P2, [k2, p2] twice.

Rows 3–6: Rep [Rows 1 and 2] twice.

Bind off.

Sew shoulder seams.

Sleeves

With MC, cast on 14 sts.

Row 1: K2, *p2, k2; rep from * across.

Row 2: P2, *k2, p2; rep from * across.

Rows 3–14: Rep [Rows 1 and 2] 6 times. Cut MC.

With CC, knit 3 rows.

Bind off.

Rep for other sleeve.

Finishing

Sew sleeve seams. Sew sleeves in shirt.

Pull right front ¾ inch across left front and sew on snap to close.

Diaper Cover

With MC, cast 8 sts.

Work in garter st (knit every row) until piece measures 2 inches—crotch formed.

Row 1: Cast on 15 sts, knit across cast-on sts and crotch, cast on 15 sts—38 sts.

Row 2: Knit across.

Row 3: *K2, p2; rep from * to last 2 sts, end k2.

Row 4: P2, *k2, p2; rep from * across.

Rows 5 and 6: Rep Rows 3 and 4.

Bind off.

Fold ends of rib tog to meet at center back and sew to cast-on edge of crotch. Sew snap at top of waist.

Booties

With MC, cast on 16 sts.

Rows 1–3: *K2, p2; rep from * across.

Row 4: K2, p2, k2, k2tog, p2tog, k2, p2, k2—14 sts.

Row 5: K2, p2, [p3tog] twice, k2, p2—10 sts.

Row 6: Knit across.

Bind off.

Sew back and bottom seam.

Cap

With MC, cast on 40 sts.

Row 1: Knit across.

Rows 2–8: *K2, p2; rep from * across.

Row 9: *K2tog, p2tog; rep from * across—20 sts.

Rows 10–13: *K1, p1; rep from * across.

Row 14: *K2tog; rep from * across—10 sts.

Cast on 8 sts, bind off 8 sts. Cut yarn leaving long end. Weave end through rem sts, and pull tight to secure. Sew back seam.

Jumper Sleeper

Wind small amount of MC into second ball, set aside.

Wind small amount of CC into second ball. Cast on 18 sts with each CC ball for legs.

Rows 1–3: Working both legs at once with separate balls of yarn, knit across both legs. Cut both balls of CC.

Row 4 (RS): Working both legs with separate balls of MC, knit across.

Row 5: Purl across.

Rows 6–13: Rep [Rows 4 and 5] 4 times.

Row 14 (joining row): *K1, kfb, k14, kfb, k1, with same ball of yarn; rep from * once more—40 sts. Cut 2nd ball of yarn.

Row 15: Purl across.

Row 16: Knit across.

Rows 17–30: Rep [Rows 15 and16] 7 times.

Row 31: P8, bind off 4 sts for armhole, p16 (includes st on needle after bind-off), bind off 4 sts for armhole, p8 (includes st on needle after bind-off)—32 sts.

Row 32: K8, cast on 6 sts, k2tog, k12, k2tog, cast on 6 sts, k8—42 sts.

Row 33: P14, p2tog, p10, p2tog, p14—40 sts.

Row 34: K1, [k2tog, k1] 13 times—27 sts. Cut MC.

Rows 35 and 36: With CC, knit across.

Bind off.

Sleeves

Beg at top of sleeve and working both sleeves at once, with MC, cast on 14 sts with each of 2 balls of yarn.

Row 1: Knit across.

Row 2: Purl across.

Rep Rows 1 and 2 until sleeves measures 1 inch. Cut MC. With CC, knit 3 rows. Bind off.

Finishing

Sew inner leg and crotch seam. Sew back seam from crotch toward neck for 1 inch. Sew snap at top opening.

Sew sleeve seams and sew in armholes.

Blanket

With MC, cast on 30 sts.

Border

Knit 5 rows.

Center

Row 1 (WS): K5, p20, k5.

Row 2 (RS): Knit across.

Rep Rows 1 and 2 until blanket measures 3 inches.

Border

Knit 5 rows.

Bind off.

Gather one end of blanket and tie with ribbon. ❖

Here Comes the Bride

Designs by Sue Childress

Skill Level
 EASY

Size
Fits 5-inch doll

Materials
- Omega Crys (sock weight; 68% acrylic/32% polyester; 287 yds/ 40g per ball): 1 ball white #200
- Size 2 (2.75mm) needles or size needed to obtain gauge
- 2 snaps
- 3 white ribbon roses
- 1 white satin bow with pearl
- ¾ yard ⅛-inch-wide red ribbon
- 3 inches ⅝-inch-wide white ribbon
- Small amount red tulle
- Sewing needle and matching thread

Gauge
8 sts = 1 inch in St st.
To save time, take time to check gauge.

Special Abbreviations
Knit in front and back (kfb): Inc 1 by knitting in front and then in back of next st.

Slip, knit 2 together, pass (sk2p): Slip next st, k2tog, pass slipped st over k2tog to dec 2 sts.

Dress
Skirt
Cast on 115 sts.

Rows 1 and 2: Knit across.

Row 3: K1, *yo, ssk, k1, k2tog, yo, k1; rep from * across.

Row 4: Purl across.

Row 5: K2, *yo, sk2p, yo, k3; rep from * to last 5 sts, yo sk2p, yo, k2.

Row 6: Purl across.

Rep [Rows 3–6] 6 times.

Bodice
Row 1: K3, *k2tog, k2; rep from * across—87 sts.

Row 2: P1, *p2tog; rep from * across—44 sts.

Row 3: K9, bind off 4 sts for armhole, k18 (includes st on needle after bind-off), bind off 4 sts for armhole, k9 (includes st on needle after bind-off)—36 sts.

Row 4: P9, cast on 6 sts, p18, cast on 6 sts, p9—48 sts.

Row 5: K15, [k2tog, k1] 6 times, k15—42 sts.

Row 6: P12, [p2tog] 9 times, p12—33 sts.

Row 7: Knit across.

Bind off.

Sleeves
Cast on 19 sts.

Row 1: Knit across.

Row 2: K1, *yo, ssk, k1, k2tog, yo, k1; rep from * across.

Row 3: Purl across.

Row 4: K2, *yo, sk2p, yo, k3; rep from * to last 5 sts, yo, sk2p, yo, k2.

Row 5: Purl across.

Rows 6–9: Rep Rows 2–5.

Row 10: [K1, k2tog] twice, k7, [k2tog, k1] twice—15 sts.

Knit 3 rows. Bind off.

Finishing
Sew sleeve seam. Sew sleeve to bodice.

Sew back seam of dress to within 1 inch of neck edge. Sew snap at neck edge.

Panties
Wind small amount of yarn for second ball. Cast on 16 sts with each ball of yarn.

Rows 1 (RS)–3: Working both legs at once with separate balls, knit across both legs.

Row 4: *K1, kfb, k12, kfb, k1; rep from * across 2nd leg.

Row 5 (joining row): With first ball, knit across both legs—36 sts. Cut 2nd ball of yarn.

Rows 6–14: Knit across.

Rows 15–18: *K2, p2; rep from * across.

Bind off in pat.

Fold ends of rows tog at center back and sew to cast-on edge of crotch. Sew back seam for ½ inch. Sew snap at waist.

Shoes
Cast on 18 sts.

Row 1: Knit across.

Row 2: K6, [k2, kfb] 3 times, k6—21 sts.

Row 3: K6, [p3tog] 3 times, k6—15 sts.

Row 4: K5, p2tog, p1, p2tog, k5—13 sts.

Rows 5–7: Knit across.

Bind off.

Sew bottom and back seams.

Headpiece
Cast on 40 sts.

Row 1: Knit across.

Rows 2–6: *K2, p2; rep from * across.

Bind off in pat.

Sew ends tog. Sew bow at front. Set aside.

Cast on 37 sts.

Row 1: Knit across.

Row 2: K1, *yo, ssk, k1, k2tog, yo, k1; rep from * across.

Row 3: Purl across.

Row 4: K2, *yo, sk2p, yo, k3; rep from * to last 5 sts, yo, sk2p, yo, k2.

Row 5: Purl across.

Rep [Rows 2–5] 5 more times.

Next row: K1, *k2tog; rep from * across—18 sts.

Next row: Knit across.

Bind off.

Sew bound-off edge to back half of headband.

Bouquet
Gather a 3-inch piece of ⅝-inch ribbon to make a circle for base of bouquet. Make small circle of tulle and sew on top of ribbon. Sew 3 ribbon roses as desired on top of tulle. Sew pieces of ⅛-inch ribbon to back making a small loop that fits around the hand. Tie ends of ribbon with overhand knot. ❖

What a Handsome Groom

Designs by Frances Hughes

Skill Level

 EASY

Size
Fits 5-inch doll

Materials
- Omega Crys (sock weight; 68% acrylic/ 32% polyester; 287 yds/40g per ball): 25 yds white #200 (A); 10 yds red #241 (B)
- Fingering weight yarn: 100 yds black (MC)
- Size 2 (2.75mm) needles or size needed to obtain gauge
- 3 snaps
- 2 pearls (3cm) or small buttons
- ¼ yd ⅛-inch-wide black ribbon
- Sewing needle and matching thread
- Small amount red and green embroidery floss for flower
- Embroidery needle

1 SUPER FINE

Gauge
8 sts = 1 inch in St st.
To save time, take time to check gauge.

Special Abbreviations
Increase (inc): Inc by knitting on RS or purling on WS in front and back of next st.

Make 1 (M1): Inc by inserting LH needle under horizontal strand between last st worked and next st on LH needle, k1-tbl.

Pattern Note
Wind MC into 2 balls before starting.

Shirt

Cummerbund
With B, cast on 38 sts, knit 3 rows. Cut B.

Body
Row 1: With A, knit across.

Row 2: K2, purl to last 2 sts, end k2.

Rows 3–6: Rep [Rows 1 and 2] twice.

Row 7: K8, bind off 5 for armhole, k12 (includes st on needle after bind off), bind off 5 for armhole, k8 (includes st on needle after bind off)—28 sts.

Row 8: K2, p6, cast on 7 sts, p12, cast on 7 sts, p6, k2—42 sts.

Row 9: Knit across.

Row 10: *K2, k2tog; rep from * across to last 2 sts, end k2—32 sts.

Row 11: Knit across.

Bind off.

Sleeve

Row 1 (RS): With RS facing and starting at center underarm, working in bound-off and cast-on sts around armhole, with A, pick up and knit 16 sts.

Row 2: Purl across.

Row 3: Knit across.

Bind off.

Rep for 2nd sleeve.

Sew 1 snap at neck edge and another at waist edge.

Referring to photo, make a bow tie from black ribbon by folding and stitching at neck. Add 2 small beads or buttons to center front of cummerbund/shirt.

For Boutonniere: Embroider French knot for rose and 2 small leaves in green.

Trousers

Legs

Cast on 18 sts with each ball of MC.

Working both legs at once with separate balls of yarn, knit 2 rows for cuff.

Row 1 (RS): Knit across.

Row 2: Purl across.

Rows 3–10: Rep [Rows 1 and 2] 4 times.

Torso

Row 1 (joining row): With first ball of yarn, *k1, inc, k14, inc, k1; * rep across 2nd leg to join—40 sts. Cut 2nd ball of yarn.

Row 2: Purl across.

Row 3: Knit across.

Row 4: Purl across.

Rows 5–8: Rep [Rows 3 and 4] twice.

Row 9: *K6, k2tog; rep from * across—35 sts.

Rows 10 and 11: Knit across.

Bind off.

Sew inside leg seam and ½ inch along center back. Sew snap at waistline.

Jacket

Back

Cast on 3 sts with each ball of MC for tux tails.

Row 1: Working both tails at once with separate balls of yarn, knit across.

Row 2 (RS): Inc, knit across first tail; knit to last st on 2nd tail; inc—4 sts on each tail.

Row 3: Inc, purl to last st on first tail, k1; k1, purl to last st on 2nd tail, inc—5 sts on each tail.

Rows 4–9: Rep [Rows 2 and 3] 3 times—11 sts on each tail.

Row 10 (joining row): With first ball, knit across both tails—22 sts. Cut 2nd ball of yarn.

Row 11: Purl across.

Row 12: Knit across.

Rows 13 and 14: Rep Rows 11 and 12.

Row 15: Cast on 8 sts for sleeve, purl across, cast on 8 sts for sleeve—38 sts.

Row 16: Knit across.

Row 17: K2, purl to last 2 sts, end k2.

Rows 18–21: Rep [Rows 16 and 17] twice.

Row 22: Knit across.

Bind off.

Front

Cast on 12 sts with each ball of MC and working both fronts at once with separate balls of yarn, knit 1 row for border.

Row 1 (RS): Knit across.

Row 2: P10, k2 on first front; k2, p10 on second front.

Rows 3–6: Rep [Rows 1 and 2] twice.

Row 7: Cast 8 sts for sleeve, k12 on first front, k12, cast on 8 sts for sleeve—20 sts on each front.

Row 8: *K2, p16, k2; rep across 2nd front.

Row 9: Knit across.

Rows 10–13: Rep [Rows 8 and 9] twice.

Bind off.

With RS facing sew shoulder seams, leaving 6 sts at both neck edges unused for collar. Sew underarm sleeves and side seams.

Collar

Note: WS of jacket is RS of collar.

Row 1 (RS): With WS of jacket facing and MC and beg at left center front, pick up and knit 6 sts along left front neck edge, 1 st at shoulder seam, 1 st in each bound-off st at center back, 1 st at shoulder seam and 6 sts across right front.

Row 2: Purl across.

Row 3: Inc, knit to last st, inc.

Row 4: Purl across.

Rows 5–12: Rep [Rows 3 and 4] 4 times.

Bind off.

Shoes

With MC cast on 17 sts.

Row 1: K7, [k1, M1] 3 times, k7—20 sts.

Row 2: Purl across.

Row 3: K9, [k1, M1] twice, k9—22 sts.

Row 4: P7 [p2tog] 4 times, p7—18 sts.

Row 5: K6, [k2tog] 3 times, k6—15 sts.

Bind off.

Sew back and bottom seam. ❖

Maid of Honor

Designs by Sue Childress

Skill Level

■■□□ EASY

Size
Fits 5-inch doll

Materials
- Omega Crys (sock weight; 68% acrylic/ 32% polyester; 287 yds/40g per ball): 75 yds purple #259 (A), 50 yds black #202 (B), and 10 yds white #200 (C)
- Size 2 (2.75mm) needles or size needed to obtain gauge
- 3 snaps
- 2 red ribbon roses
- Sewing needle and matching thread

1 SUPER FINE

Gauge
8 sts = 1 inch in St st.
To save time, take time to check gauge.

Special Abbreviation
Knit in front and back (kfb): Inc by knitting in front and back of next st.

Dress
With A, cast on 122 sts.

Rows 1–7: Knit across.

Row 8: P2, *p2tog, p1; rep from * across—82 sts.

Row 9: Knit across.

Row 10: *P1, p2tog; rep from * across to last st, p1—55 sts.

Row 11: Knit across.

Rows 12 and 13: Rep Rows 10 and 11—37 sts.

Row 14: Purl across.

Row 15: Knit across.

Rows 16–19: Rep [Rows 14 and 15] twice.

Rows 20–23: Knit across.

Row 24: K7, bind off 4 sts for armhole, k15 (includes st on needle after bind-off), bind off

4 sts for armhole, k7 (includes st on needle after bind-off)—29 sts.

Row 25: K7, cast on 4 sts, k15, cast on 4 sts, k7—37 sts.

Rows 26 and 27: Knit across.

Bind off.

Sew back seam from bottom of ruffle to waist. Sew snap at top of bodice.

Panties

With C, cast on 38 sts.

Rows 1–12: Knit across.

Row 13: Bind off 13 sts, k12 (includes st on needle after bind-off) for crotch, bind off rem sts. Fasten off.

Join yarn in first crotch st.

Knit 18 rows for crotch. Bind off.

Fold ends of rows tog at center back and sew to edge of crotch. Sew snap at waist.

Shoes

With B, cast on 17 sts.

Row 1: Knit across.

Row 2: K7, kfb of each of next 3 sts, k7—20 sts.

Row 3: K8, [k2tog] twice, k8—18 sts.

Row 4: K6, [p3tog] twice, k6—14 sts.

Rows 5 and 6: Knit across.

Change to white and knit 4 rows.

Bind off.

Sew back and bottom seam.

Headband

With B, cast on 40 sts.

Row 1: Knit across.

Rows 2 and 3: With white, *k2, p2; rep from * across.

Row 4: With black, *k2, p2; rep from * across.

Bind off.

Sew ends tog and sew rose over seam.

Cape

With B, cast on 28 sts.

Row 1: Knit across.

Row 2: *K2, kfb; rep from * across to last st, end k1—37 sts.

Rows 3–5: Knit across.

Row 6: K2, *kfb, k2; rep from * across to last st, end k1—49 sts.

Rows 7–9: Knit across.

Row 10: K2, *kfb, k2; rep from * across to last st, end k1—65 sts.

Rows 11 and 12: Knit across.

Bind off.

Sew snap at neckline. Sew rose over snap. ❖

Moses Basket & Layette

Designs by Sue Childress

Skill Level

 ■■□□ EASY

Size

Fits 5-inch doll

Materials

- Omega Crys (sock weight; 68% acrylic/ 32% polyester; 287 yds/40g per ball): 100 yds pastel yellow #231 (MC); 75 yds carousel variegated #263 (CC)
- Sport weight yarn: 50 yds brown
- Size 2 (2.75mm) needles or size needed to obtain gauge

- Size 3 (3.25mm) 16-inch circular needle or size needed to obtain gauge
- Stitch markers
- 2 snaps
- 2 white bows with pearl
- Sewing needle and matching thread
- Brown plastic canvas, at least 9 inches x 7 inches
- Small amount polyester fiberfill

Gauge

8 sts = 1 inch in St st on smaller needle.
5 sts = 1 inch in St st on larger needle.
To save time, take time to check gauge.

Special Abbreviation

Knit in front and back (kfb): Inc by knitting in front and back of next st.

Pattern Stitch

Diamond Brocade (multiple of 8 sts + 1)

Row 1 (RS): K4, *p1, k7; rep from * across to last 5 sts, end p1, k4.

Row 2: P3, *k1, p1, k1, p5; rep from * to last 6 sts, end k1, p1, k1, p3.

Row 3: K2, *p1, k3; rep from * across to last 3 sts, end p1, k2.

Row 4: P1, *k1, p5, k1, p1; rep from * across.

Row 5: *P1, k7; rep from * to last st, p1.

Row 6: Rep Row 4.

Row 7: Rep Row 3.

Row 8: Rep Row 2.

Rep Rows 1–8 for pat.

Shirt

With CC, cast on 38 sts.

Rows 1 (RS) and 2: Knit

Row 3: K2, *p2, k2; rep from * across.

Row 4: P2, *k2, p2; rep from * across.

Rows 5–8: Rep [Rows 3 and 4] twice.

Right front

Row 1 (RS): K2, [p2, k2] twice—10 sts.

Row 2: P2, [k2, p2] twice.

Rows 3–6: Rep [Rows 1 and 2] twice.

Bind off.

Back

With RS facing, join CC in next st.

Row 1: P2, [k2, p2] 4 times—18 sts.

Row 2: K2, [p2, k2] 4 times.

Rows 3–6: Rep [Rows 1 and 2] twice.

Bind off.

Left front

With RS facing, join yarn in next st.

Row 1: K2, [p2, k2] twice—10 sts.

Row 2: P2, [k2, p2] twice.

Rows 3–6: Rep [Rows 1 and 2] twice.

Bind off.

Sew shoulder seams. Sew snap at waist.

Panties

With CC, cast on 44 sts.

Knit 3 rows.

Work 5 rows in K2, P2 Rib.

Bind off 18 sts, k8 (includes st rem on needle after bind-off) for crotch, bind off rem sts. Cut yarn.

Join yarn in first crotch st.

Purl 20 rows.

Bind off.

Fold ends of rows tog at center back and sew to edge of crotch. Sew snap at top.

Booties

With CC, cast on 15 sts.

Row 1: Knit across.

Row 2: K2, p2, k2, kfb of each of next 3 sts, p2, k2, p2—18 sts.

Row 3: [K2, p2] twice, k2tog, [k2, p2] twice—17 sts.

Row 4: K2, p2, k2, p1, p3tog, p3, k2, p2—15 sts.

Rows 5 and 6: Knit across.

Bind off.

Sew bottom and back seams.

Headband

With CC, cast on 40 sts.

Row 1: *K2, p2; rep from * across.

Rows 2–4: Rep Row 1.

Bind off.

Sew ends tog and sew on ribbon bow.

Moses Basket

Bottom

With circular needle and brown, cast on 42 sts.

Knit 30 rows.

Sides

Next rnd: Working in ends of rows along side, pick up and knit 16 sts, working along cast-on edge, pick up and knit 42 sts across, working in ends of rows along other side, pick up and knit 16 sts, place marker and join to work in rnds—116 sts.

Next rnd: Knit around.

Next rnd: *K2, p2; rep from * around.

Rep last rnd 9 times.

Bind off.

Finishing

Cut 2 pieces of plastic canvas 9 inches x 1½ inches. Sew shorter sides tog to form oval. Using bottom of basket for pat, cut 1 piece of plastic the same size. Stitch oval piece around edge of bottom piece. Insert plastic in to basket and turn top of ½ inch of ribbing down over edge of plastic and stitch on inside.

Pillow

With MC, cast on 25 sts.

Knit 1 row.

Work [Rows 1–8 of Diamond Brocade pat] 7 times.

Bind off.

Fold in half with WS tog, sew 2 sides, leaving 3rd side open. Turn to RS, stuff with polyester fiberfill and sew 3rd side. Tack bow in one corner.

Blanket

With MC, cast on 65 sts.

Knit 4 rows.

Next row: K4, place marker, work Row 1 of Diamond Brocade pat to last 4 sts, place marker, k4.

Continue in established pat working sts between markers in Diamond Brocade pat and rem sts in garter st, until 9 reps of Diamond Brocade pat are complete.

Knit 4 rows.

Bind off. ❖

Sailor Boy

Designs by Frances Hughes

Skill Level

 EASY

Size

Fits 5-inch doll

Materials

- Omega Crys (sock weight; 68% acrylic/ 32% polyester; 287 yds/40g per ball): 50 yds white #200 (MC), 25 yds royal blue #214 (CC)
- Size 2 (2.75mm) straight and double-point needles or size needed to obtain gauge
- 2 snaps
- Sewing needle and matching thread

Gauge

8 sts = 1 inch in St st.
To save time, take time to check gauge.

Special Abbreviations

Increase (inc): Inc by knitting on RS or purling on WS in front and back of next st.

Make 1 (M1): Inc by inserting LH needle under horizontal strand between last st worked and next st on LH needle, k1-tbl.

Romper

Leg

Wind small amount of CC into second ball. Cast on 17 sts with each ball.

Working both legs at once with separate balls of yarn, knit 3 rows. Cut CC.

Body

Row 1 (RS): With MC, knit across both legs—34 sts.

Row 2: *P1, inc; rep from * across to last 2 sts, p2—50 sts.

Row 3: K1, inc, k22, inc in next 2 sts, k22, inc, k1—54 sts.

Row 4: Purl across.

Row 5: Knit across.

Row 6: Purl across.

Rows 7–14: Rep [Rows 5 and 6] 4 times.

Row 15: *K1, k2tog; rep from * across—36 sts.

Row 16: Purl across.

Row 17: K1, k2tog, k13, [k2tog] twice, k13, k2tog, k1—32 sts.

Row 18: P7, bind off 4 sts for armhole, p10 (includes st on needle after bind-off), bind off 4 sts for armhole, p7 (includes st on needle after bind-off)—24 sts.

Row 19: K7, cast on 6 sts, k10, cast on 6 sts, k7—36 sts.

Row 20: *K4, k2tog; rep from * across—30 sts.

Rows 21 and 22: Knit across.

Bind off knitwise.

Sleeve
Beg at underarm bind-off, with MC and dpn, pick up and knit 14 sts around sleeve opening. Divide sts evenly on 2 dpns. Do not join, work back and forth in rows.

Row 1: Purl across.

Row 2: Knit across.

Row 3: Purl across.

Rows 4 and 5: Rep Rows 2 and 3. Cut MC.

With CC, knit 3 rows.

Bind off.

Rep for 2nd sleeve.

Finishing
Sew inner leg and crotch seam. Sew center back, leaving 1½ inches from bound-off edge open. Sew snap at neck edge.

Sew underarm seam.

Shoes
With CC, cast on 17 sts.

Row 1 (RS): K7, [k1, M1] 3 times, k7—20 sts.

Row 2: Purl across.

Row 3: K9, [k1, M1] twice, k9—22 sts. Cut CC.

Row 4: With MC, p7, [p2tog] 4 times, p7—18 sts.

Row 5: K6, [k2tog] 3 times, k6—15 sts.

Row 6: P6, p3tog, p6—13 sts.

Row 7: Knit across.

Row 8: Purl across.

Rows 9 and 10: Rep Rows 7 and 8.

Bind off. Sew back and bottom seam.

Tie
With CC, cast on 40 sts.

Row 1: Knit across.

Rows 2 and 3: With MC, knit across.

Row 4: With CC, knit across.

Bind off.

Sew snap 1 inch from tip so tie will cross.

Hat

Brim
Note: Brim is worked side to side.

With CC, cast on 4 sts.

Work in garter st (knit every row) until piece measures 4 inches. Bind off. Cut CC.

Crown
Row 1 (RS): With MC, pick up and knit 50 sts in ends of rows along one long side of brim.

Row 2: Purl across.

Row 3: Knit across.

Rows 4 and 5: Rep Rows 2 and 3.

Row 6: Purl across.

Row 7: *K4, k2tog; rep from * across to last 2 sts, end k2—42 sts.

Row 8: *P3, p2tog; rep from * to last 2 sts, end p2—34 sts.

Row 9: *K2, k2tog; rep from * to last 2 sts, end k2—26 sts.

Row 10: *P1, p2tog; rep from * to last 2 sts, end p2—18 sts.

Row 11: *K3tog, [k2tog] 3 times; rep from * once more—8 sts.

Cut MC, leaving a long tail. Weave tail through sts and draw tight to close. Sew side seam through brim.

With CC, make a French knot in center top of hat. ❖

Sailor Girl

Designs by Frances Hughes

Skill Level

 EASY

Size

Fits 5-inch doll

Materials

- Omega Crys (sock weight; 68% acrylic/
  32% polyester; 287 yds/40g per ball):
  75 yds royal blue #214 (A), 50 yds white
  #200 (B)
- Size 2 (2.75mm) needles or size needed
  to obtain gauge
- Stitch markers
- 4 snaps
- 2 (3cm) pearls for jacket
- 1 (5cm) pearl for hat
- Sewing needle and matching thread

Gauge

8 sts = 1 inch in St st.
To save time, take time to check gauge.

Special Abbreviations

Knit in front and back (kfb): Inc by knitting in front
and back of next st.

Make 1 (M1): Inc by inserting LH needle under
horizontal strand between last st worked and
next st on LH needle, k1-tbl.

Dress

With B, cast on 57 sts. Knit 2 rows. Cut B.

Row 1 (RS): With A, p1, *k3, p1; rep from * across.

Row 2: K1, *p3, k1; rep from * across.

Rows 3 and 4: With B, rep Rows 1 and 2.

Rows 5 and 6: With A, rep Rows 1 and 2. Cut A.

Rows 7–14: With B, rep [Rows 1 and 2] 4 times.

Row 15: K2, *k1, k2tog; rep from * across to last
4 sts, k4—40 sts.

Row 16: K2, purl to last 2 sts, end k2.

Row 17: Knit across.

Row 18: K2, p3, *p2tog, p2; rep from * across to
last 3 sts, end p1, k2—32 sts.

Row 19: Knit across.

Row 20: K2, purl to last 2 sts, end k2.

Row 21: K7, bind off 4 sts for armhole, k10 (includes st on needle after bind-off), bind off 4 sts for armhole, k7 (includes st on needle after bind-off)—24 sts.

Row 22: K2, p5, cast on 5 sts, p10, cast on 5 sts, p5, k2—34 sts.

Row 23: [K5, k2tog] twice, k6, [k2tog, k5] twice—30 sts.

Rows 24 and 25: Knit across.

Bind off.

Sew 1 snap at neck edge and another at waistline.

Panties
Wind small amount of A into second ball. Cast on 17 sts with each ball of yarn.

Working both legs at once with separate balls of yarn, knit 2 rows.

Row 1 (RS): With MC, knit across both legs—34 sts.

Row 2: Purl across.

Row 3: K1, kfb, k14, kfb in next 2 sts, k14, kfb, k1—38 sts.

Row 4: Purl across.

Row 5: Knit across.

Row 6: Purl across

Rows 7–14: Rep [Rows 5 and 6] 4 times.

Row 15: K2, k2tog, k9, k2tog, k8, k2tog, k9, k2tog, k2—34 sts.

Bind off.

Fold ends of rows tog at back. Sew inner leg and crotch seam and ½ inch along back seam. Sew snap at waist.

Jacket
Back
With A, cast on 20 sts.

Knit 2 rows.

Row 1 (RS): Knit across.

Row 2: Purl across.

Rows 3–12: Rep [Rows 1 and 2] 5 times.

Note: Place a marker at each end of Row 5.

Bind off.

Front
Wind small amount of A into second ball. Cast on 12 sts with each ball of yarn.

Row 1: With separate balls of yarn, knit across each front.

Row 2: P10, k2 across first front; k2, p10 across 2nd front.

Rep [Rows 1 and 2] 5 times.

Note: Two garter sts are at center front of jacket. Place a marker at side edge of Row 5.

Sew fronts to back across 5 shoulder sts on each side leaving center sts unused for collar.

Sleeve
With RS facing and A and beg at marker on side, pick up and knit 5 sts in ends of rows to shoulder seam and 5 sts from shoulder seam to marker—10 sts.

Row 1: Purl across.

Row 2: Knit across.

Rows 3 and 4: Rep Rows 1 and 2.

Row 5: With B, purl across.

Row 6: Knit across.

Rows 7 and 8: With A, rep Rows 5 and 6.

Row 9: Knit across.

Bind off.

Rep for 2nd sleeve. Sew side and sleeve seams.

Collar

Note: RS of collar is WS of jacket.

Row 1 (RS): Hold jacket with WS facing and A. Beg at front edge and leaving 2 st border unworked, pick up and knit 6 sts across front to seam, 9 sts across back to seam, 6 sts across front to 2 st border—21 sts.

Row 2: Purl across.

Row 3: Knit across.

Row 4: Purl across.

Rows 5 and 6: With B, rep Rows 3 and 4.

Rows 7 and 8: With A, rep Rows 3 and 4.

Bind off.

Sew snap at center front bottom edge. Referring to photo, sew small pearl on each front.

Shoes

With A, cast on 17 sts.

Row 1 (RS): K7, [k1, M1] 3 times, k7—20 sts.

Row 2: Purl across.

Row 3: K9, [k1, M1] twice, k9—22 sts.

Row 4: P7, [p2tog] 4 times, p7—18 sts.

Row 5: K6, [k3tog] twice, k6—14 sts.

Row 6: With B, purl.

Row 7: Knit across.

Bind off.

Hat

Brim

Note: Brim is worked side to side.

With B, cast on 4 sts.

Work in garter st (knit every row) until piece measures 4 inches. Bind off. Cut B.

Crown

Row 1 (RS): With A, pick up and knit 57 sts in ends of rows along 1 long side of brim.

Row 2 and all WS rows: Purl across.

Row 3: *K1, kfb; rep from * across to last st, k1—85 sts.

Row 5: *K4, k2tog; rep from * across to last st, end k1—71 sts.

Row 7: *K3, k2tog; rep from * across to last st, end k1—57 sts.

Row 9: *K2, k2tog; rep from * to last st, end k1—43 sts.

Row 11: *K1, k2tog; rep from * to last st, end k1—29 sts.

Row 13: *K2tog; rep from * to last st, end k1—15 sts.

Row 15: *K2tog; rep from * to last st, end k1—8 sts.

Cut yarn, leaving a long tail. Draw tail through sts and pull tightly to close, sew side seam through brim.

Sew 5cm pearl at center of hat crown. ❖

Fun in the Sun

Designs by Frances Hughes

Skill Level
 ■■□□ EASY

Size
Fits 5-inch doll

Materials
- Omega Crys (sock weight; 68% acrylic/ 32% polyester; 287 yds/40g per ball): 25 yds each white #200 (A) and bright coral #254 (B)
- Size 2 (2.75mm) needles or size needed to obtain gauge
- 2 snaps
- ¾ yd ⅛-inch-wide green ribbon
- Sewing needle and matching thread

1 SUPER FINE

Gauge
8 sts = 1 inch in St st.
To save time, take time to check gauge.

Special Abbreviations
Increase (inc): Inc by knitting on RS or purling on WS in front and back of next st.

Make 1 (M1): Inc by inserting LH needle under horizontal strand between last st worked and next st on LH needle, k1-tbl.

Sun Top
With A, cast on 80 sts.

Row 1 (RS): Knit across.

Row 2: Purl across.

Row 3: *K1, k3tog; rep from * across—40 sts.

Row 4 (eyelet row): P1, *yo, p2tog; rep from * to last st, end p1.

Row 5: Knit across.

Row 6: Purl across.

Rows 7 and 8: Rep Rows 5 and 6.

Row 9: *K2, k2tog; rep from * across—30 sts.

Row 10: Purl across.

Row 11: Knit across.

Row 12: P6, bind off 4 sts for armhole, p10 (includes st on needle after bind off), bind off 4 for armhole, p6 (includes st on needle after bind off)—22 sts.

Row 13: K6, cast on 5 sts, k10, cast on 5 sts, k6—32 sts.

Rows 14–16: Knit across.

Bind off.

Sew snap at neck edge.

Pants

Wind small amount of B into second ball. Cast on 18 sts with each ball.

Rows 1 and 2: Working both legs at once with separate balls of yarn, knit across.

Row 3: Purl across.

Row 4: *K1, [yo, k2tog] 8 times, k1; rep from * across 2nd leg.

Row 5: Purl across.

Row 6: Knit across.

Row 7: Purl across.

Row 8: *K1, inc, k14, inc, k1; rep from * across 2nd leg—20 sts on each leg.

Row 9: *P1, inc, k16, inc, p1; rep from * across 2nd leg—22 sts on each leg.

Row 10 (joining row): With first ball of yarn, knit across both legs—44 sts. Cut second ball of yarn.

Row 11: Purl across.

Row 12: Knit across.

Row 13: Purl across.

Row 14: [K4, k2tog] 7 times, k2—37 sts.

Row 15: K2, purl to last 2 sts, end k2.

Row 16: Knit across.

Row 17: K2, purl to last 2 sts, end k2.

Row 18: K3, k2tog, *k4, k2tog; rep from * across to last 2 sts, end k2—31 sts.

Row 19: Knit across.

Bind off.

Sew inner leg seam and 1 inch along center back. Sew snap at waistline. Cut 2 (10-inch) lengths of ribbon. Weave 1 length through each leg, beg and ending at side, and tie in bow. Make overhand knot at each end of ribbon and trim ends even.

Headband

With B, cast on 3 sts.

Work in garter st until piece measures 4 inches.

Bind off. Sew ends tog.

Flower

With A, cast on 32 sts.

Rows 1 and 2: Knit across.

Row 3: P2, [p3tog] 10 times—12 sts.

Row 4: *K2tog; rep from * across—6 sts.

Cut yarn leaving a long end. Draw end through sts and secure. Twist into a circle and sew edges tog.

Tie rem ribbon in bow. Make overhand knot at each end and trim ends even. Tack bow to headband. Tack flower on top of bow. ❖

Baseball Player

Designs by Frances Hughes

Skill Level
 EASY

Size
Fits 5-inch doll

Materials
- Omega Crys (sock weight; 68% acrylic/ 32% polyester; 287 yds/40g per ball): 100 yds royal blue #214 (A), 25 yds white #200 (B)
- Size 2 (2.75mm) needles or size needed to obtain gauge
- 1 snap
- 2 (⅜-inch) buttons

Gauge
8 sts = 1 inch in St st.
To save time, take time to check gauge.

Special Abbreviations
Knit in front and back (kfb): Inc by knitting in front and back of next st.

Make 1 (M1): Inc by inserting LH needle under horizontal strand between last st worked and next st on LH needle, k1-tbl.

Shirt
Front/Back
Make 2 alike

With B, cast on 18 sts.

Row 1: Knit across.

Row 2: Purl across.

Rows 3–10: Rep [Rows 1 and 2] 4 times.

Row 11: Cast on 5 sts for sleeve, knit across—23 sts.

Row 12: Cast on 5 sts for sleeve, purl across—28 sts.

Rows 13–18: Rep [Rows 1 and 2] 3 times.

Bind off.

Sew side and underarm seams. Sew 9 sts on each side for shoulder seams.

Pants

Legs
Wind small amount of A into second ball. Cast on 18 sts with each ball of yarn.

Row 1 (RS): Working both legs at once with separate balls of yarn, knit across.

Row 2: Purl across.

Rows 3–12: Rep [Rows 1 and 2] 5 times.

Torso
Row 1 (joining row): With first ball of yarn, knit across both legs. Cut 2nd ball of yarn.

Row 2: Purl across.

Row 3: Knit across.

Row 4: Purl across.

Rows 5–12: Rep [Rows 3 and 4] 4 times.

Bib
Row 1 (RS): Bind off 14, k8 (includes st on needle after bind off); turn, leaving rem sts unworked—8 sts.

Rows 2–7: Work in St st.

Shoulder Strap
Row 1 (RS): K2, turn, leaving rem sts unworked—2 sts.

Rows 2–16: K2.

Bind off.

Join yarn in next unused st on bib. Bind off 4 sts, k2 (includes st on needle after bind-off).

Rep Rows 2–16 of shoulder strap.

Join yarn to rem sts on needle and bind off.

Finishing
Sew inner leg seam and approx ½ inch up center back seam. Sew snap at top.

Referring to photo, sew 2 small buttons on each side of bib straps.

Shoes
With A, cast on 17 sts.

Row 1: K7, [k1, M1] 3 times, k7—20 sts.

Row 2: Purl across. Cut A.

Row 3: With B, k9, [k1, M1] twice, k9—22 sts.

Row 4: P7, [p2tog] 4 times, p7—18 sts.

Row 5: K6, [k3tog] twice, k6—14 sts.

Bind off.

Fold in half and sew bottom and back seam.

Cap
With 2 strands of A held tog, cast on 5 sts.

Row 1 (RS): Kfb, knit to last st, kfb—7 sts.

Rows 2 and 3: Rep Row 1—11 sts.

Row 4: Knit across. Cut 1 strand.

Row 5: Cast on 12 sts, knit across, cast on 12 sts—35 sts.

Row 6: Knit across. Cut A.

Row 7: With B, knit across.

Row 8: Purl across.

Rows 9–12: Rep [Rows 7 and 8] twice.

Row 13: *K3, k2tog; rep from * across—28 sts.

Rows 14, 16 and 18: Purl across.

Row 15: *K2, k2tog; rep from * across—21 sts.

Row 17: *K1, k2tog; rep from * across—14 sts.

Row 19: *K2tog; rep from * across—7 sts.

Cut yarn leaving long end. Weave end through rem sts and pull to tighten and secure. Sew back seam.

Referring to photo, work duplicate stitch trim on cap. ❖

House of White Birches, Berne, Indiana 46711   AnniesAttic.com

Christening Set

Designs by Frances Hughes

Skill Level
 EASY

Size
Fits 5-inch doll

Materials
- Omega Crys (sock weight; 68% acrylic/ 32% polyester; 287 yds/40g per ball): 1 ball white #200
- Size 2 (2.75mm) needles or size needed to obtain gauge
- Small stitch holders
- 2 snaps
- 2 yds ⅛-inch-wide white ribbon
- Sewing needle and matching thread

Gauge
8 sts = 1 inch in St st.
To save time, take time to check gauge.

Special Abbreviations
Increase (inc): Inc by knitting on RS or purling on WS in front and back of next st.

Make 1 (M1): Inc by inserting LH needle under horizontal strand between last st worked and next st on LH needle, k1-tbl.

Gown
Sleeve
Cast on 15 sts.

Row 1: Knit across.

Row 2 (RS): *K2, (k1, p1, k1) all in next st; rep from * across—25 sts.

Row 3: *P3tog, p2; rep from * across—15 sts.

Row 4: Knit across.

Row 5: P1, *yo, p2tog; rep from * across.

Row 6: Knit across.

Row 7: Purl across.

Row 8: Bind off 1 st, k12 (includes st on needle after bind-off), k2tog—13 sts.

Row 9: P2tog, p9, p2tog—11 sts.

Place sts on holder and set aside.

Skirt
Cast on 69 sts.

Row 1: Knit across.

Row 2 (RS): *K2, (k1, p1, k1) all in next st; rep from * across—115 sts.

Row 3: *P3tog, p2; rep from * across—69 sts.

Row 4: *K1, yo, k2tog; rep from * across.

Row 5: P1, p2tog, purl rem sts—68 sts.

Row 6: K1, p2, *k2, p2; rep from * across to last st, end k1.

Row 7: K3, *p1, yo, p1, k2; rep from * to last st, end k1—84 sts.

Row 8: K1, p2, *k3, p2; rep from * to last st, end k1.

Row 9: K3, *p3, k2; rep from * across to last st, end k1.

Row 10: K1, p2, *k3, past first st of 3 sts just worked over last 2 sts, p2; rep from * to last st, end k1—68 sts.

Rep [Rows 7–10] 7 times.

Yoke
Row 1: K2, p13, bind off 4 sts for armhole, p30 (includes st on needle after bind-off), bind off 4 sts for armhole, p13 (includes st on needle after bind-off), k2—60 sts.

Row 2 (RS joining row): Work across back as follows: [K2tog, k2] 3 times, k2tog, k1, work across first sleeve as follows: [K2tog, k3tog] 3 times; work across front of skirt as follows: [K2tog, k3tog] 6 times, work across second sleeve as follows: [k2tog, k3tog] 3 times, work across back as follows: K1, k2tog, [k2, k2tog] 3 times—46 sts.

Row 3: K2, [yo, p3tog] 14 times, yo, k2—33 sts.

Row 4: Knit across.

Row 5: K2, purl to last 2 sts, end k2.

Row 6: [K2, k2tog] 8 times, k1—25 sts.

Row 7: K2, purl to last 2 sts, k2.

Bind off.

Beg and ending at center front, weave ribbon through Row 3 (eyelet row) of yoke and tie in bow. Make overhand knot at each end of ribbon and trim ends even. Sew snap at top of neck.

Panties
Wind small amount of yarn into second ball. Cast on 16 sts with each ball.

Rows 1 and 2: Working both legs at once with separate balls of yarn, knit across.

Row 3: *P1, inc, purl to last 2 sts, inc, p1; rep from * across 2nd leg—18 sts on each leg.

Row 4 (joining row): With first ball, knit across both legs—36 sts. Cut 2nd ball.

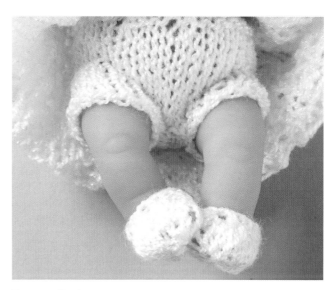

Row 5: Purl across.

Row 6: Knit across.

Row 7: Purl across.

Rows 8–13: Rep [Rows 6 and 7] 3 times.

Row 14: K2, k2tog, [k8, k2tog] 3 times, k2—32 sts.

Bind off.

Sew inner leg seam and ½ inch along center back. Sew snap at waistline.

Shoes
Cast on 17 sts.

Row 1: K7, [k1, M1] 3 times, k7—20 sts.

Row 2: Purl across.

Row 3: K9, [k1, M1] twice, k9—22 sts.

Row 4: P7, [p2tog] 4 times, p7—18 sts.

Row 5: K6, [k3tog] twice, k6—14 sts.

Bind off. Sew back and bottom seam.

Hat
Brim
Cast on 42 sts.

Row 1 (RS): *(K1, p1, k1) all in next st, k2; rep from * across—56 sts.

Row 2: *P2, p3tog; rep from * across—42 sts.

Row 3: *K1, yo, k2tog; rep from * to last st, end k1.

Row 4: Purl across.

Row 5: *K5, k2tog; rep from * across—36 sts.

Row 6: Purl across.

Row 7: Knit across.

Row 8: Purl across.

Rows 9–12: Rep Rows 7 and 8.

Crown

Row 13: *K4, k2tog; rep from * across—30 sts.

Row 14: *P3, p2tog; rep from * across—24 sts.

Row 15: *K2, k2tog; rep from * across—18 sts.

Row 16: *P1, p2tog; rep from * across—12 sts.

Cut yarn leaving a long end; draw end through sts, pull tight and secure. Sew side seam.

Weave ribbon through Row 3 and tie ends in bow.

Blanket

Lace Border

Make 2

Cast on 8 sts.

Row 1: Sl 1, k1, *yo, p2tog, (k1, p1, k1) all in next st; rep from * once more—12 sts.

Row 2: [K3, yo, p2tog] twice, k2.

Row 3: Sl 1, k1, [yo, p2tog, k3] twice.

Row 4: Bind off 2 sts, (1 st left on RH needle), yo, p2tog, bind off next 2 sts (4 sts left on RH needle), yo, p2tog, k2—8 sts.

Rep [Rows 1–4] 14 times, and then rep Rows 1–3.

Bind off. Do not cut yarn (st left on needle).

Working across top edge of lace, pick up and knit 63 sts—64 sts.

Set aside 2nd lace border for upper border.

Center

Row 1: K5, p2, *k2, p2; rep from * across to last 5 sts, end k5.

Row 2: K7, *p1, yo, p1, k2; rep from * across to last 5 sts, k5—77 sts.

Row 3: K5, p2, *k3, p2; rep from * across to last 5 sts, k5.

Row 4: K7, *p3, k2; rep from * across to last 5 sts, k5.

Row 5: K5, p2, *k3, pass first st of sts just worked over last 2 sts, p2; rep from * across to last 5 sts, end k5—64 sts.

Rep [Rows 2–5] 7 times.

Next row: K5, purl to last 5 sts, end k5.

Finishing

With center of blanket facing, place other lace border piece RS tog and knit these 2 pieces tog with 3-needle bind-off.

Referring to photo, weave ribbon through top and bottom borders. Cut 4 (8-inch) lengths of ribbon and tie each in bow. Trim ends even and tack in place in each of 4 corners. ❖

Standard Abbreviations

[ ] work instructions within brackets as many times as directed
( ) work instructions within parentheses in the place directed
** repeat instructions following the asterisks as directed
* repeat instructions following the single asterisk as directed
" inch(es)

approx approximately
beg begin/beginning
CC contrasting color
ch chain stitch
cm centimeter(s)
cn cable needle
dec decrease/decreases/decreasing
dpn(s) double-pointed needle(s)
g gram
inc increase/increases/increasing
k knit

k2tog knit 2 stitches together
LH left hand
lp(s) loop(s)
m meter(s)
M1 make one stitch
MC main color
mm millimeter(s)
oz ounce(s)
p purl
pat(s) pattern(s)
p2tog purl 2 stitches together
psso pass slipped stitch over
p2sso pass 2 slipped stitches over
rem remain/remaining
rep repeat(s)
rev St st reverse stockinette stitch
RH right hand
rnd(s) rounds
RS right side
skp slip, knit, pass stitch over—one stitch decreased

sk2p slip 1, knit 2 together, pass slip stitch over the knit 2 together—2 stitches have been decreased
sl slip
sl 1k slip 1 knitwise
sl 1p slip 1 purlwise
sl st slip stitch(es)
ssk slip, slip, knit these 2 stitches together—a decrease
st(s) stitch(es)
St st stockinette stitch/stocking stitch
tbl through back loop(s)
tog together
WS wrong side
wyib with yarn in back
wyif with yarn in front
yd(s) yard(s)
yfwd yarn forward
yo yarn over

Inches into Millimeters & Centimeters

All measurements are rounded off slightly.

inches	mm	cm	inches	cm	inches	cm	inches	cm	inches	cm
⅛	3	0.3	3	7.5	13	33.0	26	66.0	39	99.0
¼	6	0.6	3½	9.0	14	35.5	27	68.5	40	101.5
⅜	10	1.0	4	10.0	15	38.0	28	71.0	41	104.0
½	13	1.3	4½	11.5	16	40.5	29	73.5	42	106.5
⅝	15	1.5	5	12.5	17	43.0	30	76.0	43	109.0
¾	20	2.0	5½	14	18	46.0	31	79.0	44	112.0
⅞	22	2.2	6	15.0	19	48.5	32	81.5	45	114.5
1	25	2.5	7	18.0	20	51.0	33	84.0	46	117.0
1¼	32	3.8	8	20.5	21	53.5	34	86.5	47	119.5
1½	38	3.8	9	23.0	22	56.0	35	89.0	48	122.0
1¾	45	4.5	10	25.5	23	58.5	36	91.5	49	124.5
2	50	5.0	11	28.0	24	61.0	37	94.0	50	127.0
2½	65	6.5	12	30.5	25	63.5	38	96.5		

HOUSE of WHITE BIRCHES
PUBLISHERS SINCE 1947

Itty Bitty Knitties is published by DRG, 306 East Parr Road, Berne, IN 46711. Printed in USA. Copyright © 2010 DRG. All rights reserved. This publication may not be reproduced in part or in whole without written permission from the publisher.

RETAIL STORES: If you would like to carry this pattern book or any other DRG publications, visit DRGwholesale.com.

Every effort has been made to ensure that the instructions in this pattern book are complete and accurate. We cannot, however, take responsibility for human error, typographical mistakes or variations in individual work. Please visit AnniesCustomerCare.com to check for pattern updates.

ISBN: 978-1-59217-320-4
2 3 4 5 6 7 8 9

Photo Index

6

9

4

11

14

16

24

19

21

26

28